Nos Gusta Tocar Música

We Like to Play Music

DEDICATION: *For Ashe and Zac, the music in my life. And for Lee, the maestro.*
Para Ashe y Zac, la música en mi vida. Y para Lee, el maestro.

Diseño de portada: Zachary Parker
Diseño de libro: Zachary Parker, Kadak Graphics, Prescott, Arizona
Traducido al español por Jocelyn del Río

Library of Congress Cataloging-in-Publication Data:

Parker, Kate.
 [We like to play music. Spanish & English]
 Nos gusta tocar musica = We like to play music / Kate Parker ; diseno de libro Zachary Parker. -- Bi-lingual ed.
    p. cm.
 Parallel texts in Spanish and English.
 ISBN 978-1-890772-90-1 (trade paper : alk. paper)
 1. Music--Instruction and study--Juvenile. 2. Music appreciation--Juvenile literature. I. Parker, Zac. II. Title. III. Title: We like to play music.
 MT6.P19918 2009
 781.1'7--dc22
                    2008041325

HOHM PRESS
P.O. Box 2501
Prescott, AZ 86302
800-381-2700
www.hohmpress.com

Este libro fue impreso en China.

11 10 09 08 07   5 4 3 2 1

Nos Gusta Tocar Música
We Like to Play Music

Bi-Lingual Edition

KATE PARKER

Diseño de
Zac Parker

HOHM PRESS
Prescott, Arizona

Nota para Padres y Maestros

Este libro fue creado para los niños pequeños (y para el pequeño niño que hay dentro de cada uno de nosotros). Los niños demuestran tanto gusto y curiosidad con las experiencias sonoras, que nos es natural promoverlos.

Simplemente sacudir unas maracas o latas llenas de frijoles con cierto ritmo, puede deleitarle a un niño por horas. Bailar con la música favorita puede sacar tensiones y animar tanto a los pequeños como a los grandes. No tiene que cantar como Pavarotti para que un niño disfrute al escuchar su voz. Escucharle cantar lo inspira para él cante con usted ... o solo.

¡Todo el mundo puede tocar música! El tocar música es una manera en que las personas se relacionan y disfrutan la mutua compañía. Las fotografías en este libro son de niños de distintas edades, utilizando instrumentos diversos y tocando música. Enseñan a adultos y a niños disfrutando juntos la música.

Pueden leer o cantar este libro con un ritmo sencillo inventado por ustedes. Pueden hablar sobre las imágenes. Descubra como a los niños les gustaría jugar con instrumentos, movimientos o sonidos. Ponga pués el libro de lado mientras "bailan, cantan y juegan". El texto es suficientemente fácil para ser memorizado. Facilita que los niños se lo aprendan y lo repitan. ¡Gócenlo!

Note to Parents and Teachers

This book was created for the young child (and also for the child within each of us). Small children bring so much joy and curiosity to the experience of sound that it seems only natural to encourage them.

Simply shaking maracas, or orange juice cans filled with beans, to a rhythm can delight children for hours. Dancing around to favorite music can release tension and uplift both children and adults. You don't have to sing like Pavarotti for children to love the sound of your voice. Hearing you sing inspires them to sing along … or alone.

Everyone can play music! Playing music is a way for people to connect and enjoy each other's company. The photographs in this book show a variety of children of different age groups, using different instruments and actually playing music. They show adults and children enjoying music together.

This book can be read or sung to a simple tune that you make up. Talk about the images. Find out how your child or children would like to play with instruments, movement or sound. Then put the book down while you do your own "shaking, rattling and rolling." The text is easy enough to memorize, so let your children read it back to you, again and again. Have a great time.

Nos gusta tocar.
We like to play.

Nos gusta cantar.
We like to sing.

Nos gusta sonar el tambor.

We like to drum.

Y a la campana hacer tintinear.

We like to ring.

Nos gusta bailar
Girar y dar un
brinco.

We like to
shake and rattle
and roll.

Al son de la
música
Con alma y
ritmo.

We like to
play music
with rhythm
and soul!

Nos gusta la melodía.

We like the beat.

Nos gusta el sonido.

We like the sound.

Nos gusta lento, en armonía.

We like music soft.

Nos gusta fuerte y movido.

We like music loud.

La música nos conecta a nuestro sentir.

Music connects us and shows how we feel.

**La música
nos afecta
y nos ayuda
a sanar.**

**Music affects
us and can help
us to heal.**

La música es natural.

Music is natural.

La música es algo grande.

Music is grand.

Podemos hacer la nuestra
¡Y tocar en una banda!

We can make music by joining a band!

Ven y haz tu propio sonido.

Music is special, however it's done.

**Ven y toca
!Verás que
divertido es!**

**You can make
music too,
so join in
the fun!**

OTROS TÍTULOS DE INTERÉS DE LA EDITORIAL HOHM
OTHER TITLES OF INTEREST FROM HOHM PRESS

Nos Gustan Nuestros Dientes / We Like Our Teeth

Written and Illustrated by Marcus Allsop

Bi-Lingual Versiona ISBN: 978-1-890772-89-5
papel, 32 páginas, $9,95

English ISBN: 978-890772-86-4
paper, 32 pages, $9.95

Nos Gusta Comer Bien / We Like To Eat Well

by Elyse April

Illustrations by Lewis Agrell

Español ISBN: 978-1-890772-78-9
papel, 32 páginas, $9,95

English ISBN: 978-890772-69-7
paper, 32 pages, $9.95

Nos Gusta Movernos: El Ejercicio Es Divertido / We Like To Move: Exercise Is Fun

by Elyse April
Illustrations by Diane Iverson

Español ISBN: 978-890772-65-9,
papel, 32 páginas, $9,95

English ISBN: 978-890772-60-4
paper, 32 pages, $9.95

Nos Gusta Ayudar a Cocinar / We Like To Help Cook

by Marcus Allsop
Illustrations by Diane Iverson

Español ISBN: 978-1-890772-75-8
papel, 32 páginas, $9,95

English ISBN: 978-890772-70-3
paper, 32 pages, $9.95

PEDIDOS / ORDERS: 800-381-2700; sitio web / website: www.hohmpress.com
Descuentos especiales por mayoreo. / Special discounts for bulk orders.

DOVER PICTORIAL ARCHIVE SERIES

Games & Pastimes of Childhood

JACQUES STELLA

Games & Pastimes of Childhood

ENGRAVED BY CLAUDINE BOUZONNET STELLA

Preface, translations and notes by Stanley Appelbaum

DOVER PUBLICATIONS, INC., NEW YORK

Published in Canada by General Publishing Company, Ltd.,
30 Lesmill Road, Don Mills, Toronto, Ontario.
Published in the United Kingdom by Constable and Company, Ltd.,
10 Orange Street, London WC 2.

This Dover edition, first published in 1969, is an unabridged and
unaltered facsimile republication (reproduced from a copy of the original edition) of the work published by Claudine Bouzonnet Stella,
Paris, in 1657 under the title *Les ieux [jeux] et plaisris [plaisirs]
de l'enfance*. The preface, notes and translations were written specially
for the present edition.

Games and Pastimes of Childhood belongs to the Dover Pictorial
Archive Series. Up to five illustrations from this book may be reproduced on any one project or in any single publication free and without
special permission. Wherever possible include a credit line indicating
the title and publisher of this book. Please address the publisher for
permission to make more extensive use of illustrations in this book than
that authorized above.

The republication of this book in whole is prohibited.

Standard Book Number: 486-22341-8
Library of Congress Catalog Card Number: 70-78893

Manufactured in the United States of America
Dover Publications, Inc.
180 Varick Street
New York, N. Y. 10014

Preface to the Dover Edition

Jacques Stella, who drew the pictures for *Les jeux et plaisirs de l'enfance*, was born in Lyons in 1596 and died in Paris in 1657, the year in which the book was published. The most illustrious member of an artistic family of Flemish origin active in France in the sixteenth and seventeenth centuries, he was primarily a painter of religious and historical subjects. From 1619 to 1623 he was in Florence, where he worked for the Medici; from 1623 to about 1635, in Rome, where he became a friend of Poussin. Back in Paris, with Richelieu's sponsorship Stella was named "Premier peintre du Roi."

Claudine Bouzonnet, engraver and publisher of this work, was one of Jacques' nieces and pupils; she used the family name Stella. She was born in Lyons in 1636 and died in Paris, where she had an apartment in the Louvre, in 1697. A painter herself, she is best known as an engraver, especially from drawings and paintings of Jacques Stella and Poussin.

Aside from its charm and artistic merit, *Les jeux et plaisirs* is a major source for the history of games. Games have been depicted in art since ancient times, but such purposeful collections as this are rare. A major French print cycle of thirty-six subjects published in 1587 shows people of all ages dressed in their everyday clothes. Jacques Stella's exclusive use in his cycle of nude putti playing small children's games is probably greatly indebted to the analogous series by Agostino Carracci (1557–1602). One of the rare extant prints engraved by Stella himself shows a group of nude children dancing in front of an inn with adults (clothed) looking on delightedly.

In the present volume the anonymous descriptive verses that accompany the prints have been translated freely to retain the original meter and rhyme schemes. Very brief notes have been added here and there to help pinpoint the precise variety of the game that is illustrated or to supply other explanations, but no attempt has been made to trace completely the history and ramifications of the games; for this, the reader is referred to the following works.

Bibliography

Allemagne, Henry René d', *Récréations et passe-temps,* Hachette, Paris, n.d. [1905].

————, *Sports et jeux d'adresse,* Hachette, Paris, n.d. [1903]. Both these d'Allemagne works, which evaluate Stella as a source, are profusely illustrated with historical material, including precursors, parallels and imitations of *Les jeux et plaisirs.*

Dillaye, Frédéric, *Les jeux de la jeunesse; leur origine, leur histoire et l'indication des règles qui les régissent,* Hachette, Paris, 1885.

Gomme, Alice Bertha, *The Traditional Games of England, Scotland, and Ireland,* 2 vols., originally pub. London, 1894 and 1898, reprinted by Dover, 1964. The English names assigned to the games in this volume are largely based on those in the Gomme work.

S. A.

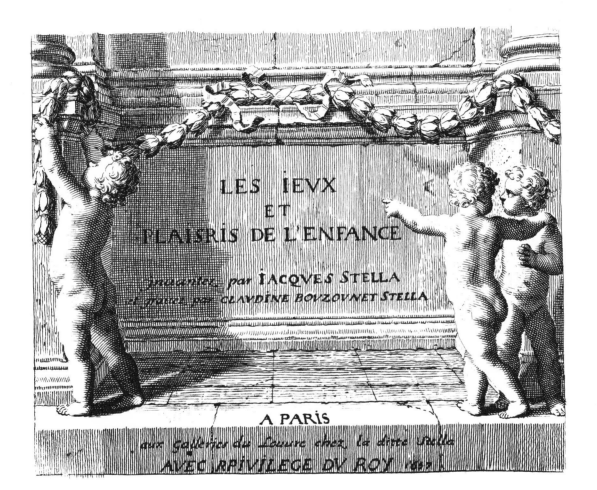

LES IEVX
ET
PLAISRIS DE L'ENFANCE

inuentez par IACQVES STELLA
& grauez par CLAVDINE BOVZONNET STELLA

A PARIS
aux galleries du Louure chez la dite Stella
AVEC RPIVILEGE DV ROY 1657

1 CHASING BUTTERFLIES

This baby in the cradle smirks
To see how hard his brother works
For such a silly sort of thing:
Though he can hardly walk as yet,
He seriously hopes to get
A butterfly that's on the wing.

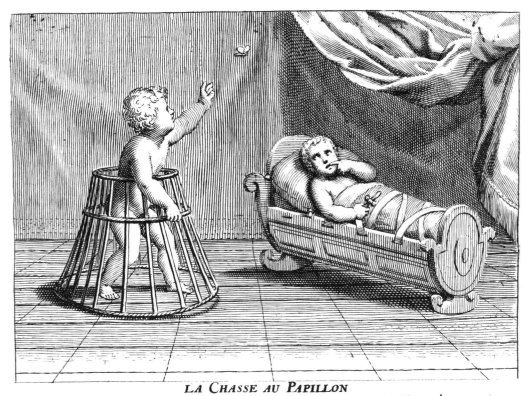

LA CHASSE AU PAPILLON

Cet Enfant rit dans Son Berceau
de voir Son frere tout en eau
pour vne chose Si frivole ;

Et qu'en vain il veuille tascher
(Bien qu'a peine il puisse marcher)
de prendre vn Papillon qui vole.

2   THE HOBBYHORSE

Some of these happy tykes are smitten
With love for sparrow, pup or kitten,
While some by love of dolls are swayed.
This other, on a childish whim,
Carries, in this fine promenade,
The horse that ought to carry him.

LE DADA

Chacun fait icy son esbat   G cet autre qu'on voit trotter
d'vn moineau, d'vn chien ou d'vn chat,   porte, en cette belle equippée,
d'vn poupart, ou d'vne poupeé,   le cheval qui le doit porter.

2

3   THE WHIPPING TOP

This whipping top, unkindly used,
Although by lashes stung and bruised,
Turns a deaf ear and starts to drowse;
And so these toddlers are impressed
That whips, which ought to wake and rouse,
Now serve to set their tops at rest.

This type of top, kept moving by whiplashes, is known
from antiquity. In both French and English, "sleeping"
refers to the apparent immobility of a balanced top rotat-
ing at maximum speed.

LE SABOT

Ce Sabot ainsy mal traitté,
quoy qu'il Soit rudement fouëtté,
S'endort et fait la Sourde oreille ;

& ce qui Surprend ces marmots
est que le fouët, qui les reveille
Sert pour endormir leurs Sabots.

3

4 THE SEESAW

The children at the upper end
Believe they never will descend,
But down they plummet by and by.
Fortune is changeable, and so
All worldly favors come and go:
When one man's low, another's high.

LA BALANÇOIRE

Ceux cy qui tiennent le haut bout   La chance tourne, & c'est ainsy
pensent estre au dessus de tout,   que tout roule en ce monde cy,
mais leur descente sera prompte ;   ou l'vn descend quant l'autre monte

4

5   THE MASK

This master of inventive fraud
Has his poor comrades overawed—
They think the mask's a real live satyr;
And is it not a great surprise
That what should be a laughing matter
Brings tears of terror to their eyes!

This subject dates back to Roman frescos.

LE MASQUE

Que ce gaillard est jnventif
d'effrayer ce pauvre craintif
avec Son masque de Satire ;

& ne doit on pas admirer
que, ce qui le doit faire rire,
l'espouvante, et le fait pleurer 5

6 PUSH-PIN

As these two children gaily run,
Their pinwheels by the wind are spun.
The other tots, on grassy seats,
Of animation all bereft,
Try, after several defeats,
To save the pins they still have left.

The object was to get one pin to cross another; the pins were also the stakes in the game. The expression *tirer son épingle du jeu* (to withdraw one's pin from the game) is still used in French to mean "to cut one's losses" or "to be well out of a bad situation."

LE IEU DES ESPINGLES

Cependant que ces mignonets   ne S'animent pas pour vn peu ,
mettent au vent leurs moulinets ; pretendans, apres quelque perte ,
d'autres assis Sur l'herbe verte   tirer leurs espingles du Ieu .   6

7 THE SLED

This commoner, as if a tsar,
Is drawn in his triumphal car.
Of falls or spills he has no dread;
For if an accidental stumble
Should send him toppling from his sled,
He hasn't very far to tumble.

LE TRAISNEAU

Ce Populo, comme vn Cesar,
Se fait trainer dedans son Char,
Sans avoir crainte qu'il ne averse;

Car en tout cas, si quelque saut
le fait tomber à la renverse,
ce ne sera pas de fort haut.

7

8 Soap Bubbles

Here children scrap and suffer troubles
For nothing greater than soap bubbles,
As though for guineas, pounds and pence.
And yet we see among adults
The same ado, the same results
For things of much less consequence.

LES BOUTEILLES DE SAVON

Ceux cy se gourment tout de bon
pour ces Bouteilles de Savon
Comme si cestoit des Pistoles ;

Mais souvent parmy les grans
on avoit naistre des differens
pour milles choses plus frivoles. 8

9   THE SWING

The swing gives them so much delight
That they could stay there day and night.
Be careful not to slip—alas!
For when one falls from where he sits,
If his behind were made of glass
It must be broken into bits.

L'ESCARPOLETE

l'Escarpolete est vn deduit
à passer le Jour et la Nuit;
mais garde de tomber par terre,

Car quand vn drosle est renuersé,
si son derriere estoit de verre,
il pouroit bien estre cassé.

9

10   Pot Breaking

In this, a roughneck type of sport,
One fellow of the bolder sort
Prepares to deal some mighty smashes.
He'll get a soaking, like as not,
And, what is worse, the broken pot
Could crack his head when down it crashes.

La course du pot could be translated as "Pot Running."
Another French name for the game, cited by the author
Paul Scarron (1610–1660), is *casse-pot*, "Pot Breaking."

LA COURSE DU POT

A cette course de Faquin,
on voit ce petit Maroquin
qui de bien frapper s'appreste;

Sans doute qu'il sera mouillé,
et qui pis est le Pot cassé
pouroit bien luy casser la teste.

10

11   Fire Leaping

To them it seems a wondrous treat,
Right in the heart of summer's heat,
To leap across a brushwood fire;
But if the pleasure of this game
Should last no longer than their flame,
It soon will gutter and expire.

LES PETIS FEVX

Ce leur est vne volupté
de Sauter, au cœur de l'Esté,
par dessus ces feux de bourée;

Mais si le plaisir de ce jeu
ne dure pas plus que leur feu
il sera de courte durée.

11

12 BLIND MAN'S BUFF

I'm sorry for the child who's "it,"
Seeing how hard he's being hit—
His friend is strong and isn't shy.
Maybe he'll even up the score;
Some doorman surely will reply
If he keeps pounding on the "door."

LE COLIN MAILLARD

Ie plains fort ce Colin Maillard
en voyant cet autre gaillard
qui ne frappe pas de main morte

mais peut estre il luy revaudra;
et sil heurte tant à la porte
quelque portier luy repondra.

12

13   SHUTTLECOCK

If these two aren't worth their salt,
The shuttlecock may be at fault,
Or else the battledore's unsound.
And isn't it a comic theme,
The labor of this equine team
To drag the coach along the ground?

With a net and some stricter rules, this game became
badminton.

LE VOLANT

Si ces Ioueurs n'adressent bien
c'est que le Volant ne vaut rien
ou que la Palette est percée :

Mais qui ne riroit des travaux
que Souffrent ces petis Chevaux;
pour traisner cette Carosséé.

13

14 NINE HOLES

This tender child, whose foremost goal
Is filling up the center hole,
Uses his brains and skill and might;
But it may happen nonetheless
That purely from capricious spite
The ball will ruin his success.

This is also known as a board game. In the clearest description, the purpose was to get the marble or ball into all the holes in succession. In the present poem the (immediate?) aim is to fill the center hole.

LA FOSSETTE

Ce mignon, pour trouver lieu
d'atteindre à celle du milieu,
vse d'adresse et d'artifice ;

Il pouroit bien estre pourtant
que l'Estœuf, par belle malice,
ne fera pas ce qu'il pretend.

14

15 CASTLES

At heaps of marbles he takes aim
(They're known as "castles" in the game)
And tries to crush a castle's walls.
It makes no difference which it is:
The spoils of war are fairly his
As soon as any castle falls.

Played with marbles or cherrystones heaped in pyramids
of one on three.

LA RANGETTE

Ils visent tous à ces monceaux,   *Quel qu'il soit il n'importe pas,*
qu'entre eux ilz nôment des chasteaux,   *car tout est pris de bône guerre*
pour en jetter quelqu'un par terre;   *pourveu qu'on en mettz vn à bas*

15

Although these cherrystones for them
Are worth a precious diadem,
These hopeful youngsters bravely toil
To throw their treasures in a pit;
But I'd say on the face of it,
They're being sown in barren soil.

LA FOSSETTE AUX NOYAUX

Quoy qu'ilz estiment ces Noyaux les jette en terre asseurement,
autant que de riches Ioyaux , mais j'apprehende aucunement
ce Cadet qui d'espoir se flatte qu'il ne les Seme en terre jngratte. 16

17 NINE MEN'S MORRIS AND THE KITE

The morris and "avoid-the-square"
Are all their business and their care;
They strive to play with expertise.
The other infant with his kite
Runs breathlessly and gives the breeze
A plaything for its own delight.

In Nine Men's Morris (being played at the lower left; also known as Morris, Merels, Merelles and Merrils) the object was to get three men in a row (compare Tick-tacktoe). In *franc du carreau* ("free of the square"; diagram at lower right) the pieces pitched were not supposed to touch any line.

LA MERELLE, & LE CERF VOLANT

La Merelle et Franc du quareau
Sont icy mis sur le bureau,
chacun a bien joüer prend peine;

& l'autre avec son Cerf Volant
va courant a perte d'haleine
pour fournir d'vn joüet au Vent.

17

18 HOPSCOTCH

The child that's hopping in this game
(In imitation of the lame)
Follows the lines traced on the ground.
He may be laboring in vain,
For if he goes beyond the bound
His stake becomes his rival's gain.

LA MARELLE A CLOCHE-PIÉ

Cet Enfant saute a Cloche-pié   Peut estre qu'il travaille en vain,
contre-faisant l'estropié   car, s'il passe outre la mesure,
par dessus cette tablature ;   Son En-jeu changera de main. 18

19 PITCHING PENNIES

It seems this lad on pleasure bent
Tosses his token or his cent
Not as he should, but in reverse.
But that boy won't end up a debtor
Who, truly mindful of his purse,
Steps backward to jump forward better.

In England the game is called Chuck-farthing. This engraving shows the distance between pitched tokens being measured with a stick; hand spans were sometimes used.

LA PATTE AVX IETTONS

Il sembleroit que ce gaillard
jette son Ietton ou son liard
au rebours de ce qu'il doit faire :

Mais au lieu de s'en escarter,
il tend tousjours à son affaire,
& recule pour mieux sauter. 19

This hefty boy adopts a stance
As if some Samson born in France;
Though larger than his chums, he's droller,
For, looking at his height, one may
Be pardoned if inclined to say
He isn't such a fearful bowler.

LES QVILLES

A voir camper ce gros garçon
il doit passer pour vn Samson
parmy ces autres petis drilles;

Mais vû sa taille, il est constant
qu'on ne sçauroit dire pourtant
qu'il soit grand abbateur de Quilles.

20

21 QUOITS

This youngster seems to run a risk
To keep the game alive and brisk,
Devising some ingenious ruse.
But playing well, his little chum
Prescribes for him some rules of thumb
Which he himself had failed to use.

These quoits are not ring-shaped. In some forms of the game, coins were to be knocked off the post. Related sports: discus throwing, horseshoes. The meaning of *l'avoir en deux* is not perfectly clear.

LE PALET

Ce cadet parest hazardeux,
& tasche pour l'avoir en deux
d'inventer quelque stratagesme :

Mais cet autre a bonne façon
de luy prescrire vne leçon
quil n'a sçeu prendre po.^r luy mesme.

22 THE SPINNING TOP

The fair lads in this company
Find it an endless source of glee
To knock their friends' tops out of play.
Their friends then suffer countless woes
To see their own tops sent astray
And taking heavy jolts and blows.

LA TOVPIE

Qúilz sont ravis ces beaux mignons   & que les autres sont dolens
alors que de leurs compagnons   de voir les leurs assujeties
ils peuvent sapper les Toupies   a souffrir ces coups violens.

22

23 HEY COCKALORUM

The boy who leaped is justified
In showing such triumphal pride,
For wondrous valor he displayed:
Through well-armed outworks first he runs,
And takes the wall by escalade,
Braving two loaded, leveled guns.

"Hey Cockalorum," another term for Leapfrog, has been used here to distinguish this plate from no. 38. In *cheval fondu* (broken-down horse) the stooping boys lined up, holding the hips of those in front, while the leaping boys jumped as far forward as possible.

LE CHEVAL FONDV

Cest à bon droit que cet Enfant,   Puisq' en des lieux si bien flanquez
en posture de triomphant,   il passe, & monte a lescalade
de sa braveure fait parade :   par dessus deux canons braquez.

23

24   HANDSTANDS

To see their sudden starts and fits,
You'd think these tots had lost their wits
And badly needed hellebore;
Yet they're as trim as they can be
If, as Pythag'ras said of yore,
A man's a topsy-turvy tree.

Hellebore was thought to cure madness.

LA CVLEBVTE

A voir leurs Soubresauts bouffons
qui ne diroit que ces Poupons
auroient bon besoin d'Ellebore ;

Leurs corps est pourtant bien dresse
Si, Selon que dit Pythagore,
l'homme est vn arbre renversé.

24

25   TOY CANNONS

Assuredly these sprightly elves,
With cannons that they've made themselves,
Will storm great forts in mighty wars:
What weapons or what mysteries
Can sooner open hostile doors
Than such petards and such great keys?

LES PETITS CANONS

Asseurement ces mirmidons
vont forcer, avec leurs Canons,
les Citadelles les plus fortes :

Car par quelle arme, ou par quel art
peut on mieux en ouvrir les portes
que par la Clef; ou le Petart.

26 WAR

These little soldiers marching out
Could put the bravest foe to rout
And place the world beneath their sway;
But since their arms are rather light,
If I interpret it aright,
They're only setting out to play.

LA GVERRE

Ce nombre de petis Soldats
pouroient donner de grans combats
G conquerir toute la terre :

Mais, estans armez de leger
leurs Equipage fait juger
qu'ilz vont à la petite guerre

20

27   TENNIS (PAUME)

Undraped, alert and debonair,
The minute they have time to spare
These boys with rackets all run riot;
And, passed among this reckless batch,
The ball, without a moment's quiet,
Knows it has surely met its match.

LA PAVME

Ainsy nuds legers et dispos
ces Enfans, des qu'ilz ont campos
vont s'escrimer de la raquette,

Ou la Balle tousjours en l'air
parmy cette trouppe jnquiette
trouve sans doute à qui parler

27

While one of them is occupied
In guessing who has tanned his hide,
His comrades give themselves free rein.
He'd think Dame Fortune much more kind
And spare himself a lot of pain
If he had eyes in his behind.

Another French name is *main chaude* (Hot Hand). The player whose face is hidden must guess who is hitting his exposed hand. This has been a popular game among children and adults for centuries. In a set of prints of the four ages of man engraved by Claudine Bouzonnet after Jacques Stella, this game represents adolescence.

LE FRAPPE MAIN

Pendant qu'vn d'eux est occupé
a deviner qui l'a frappé
les autres s'en donnent carriere ;

Ha que le Sort luy seroit doux
s'il avoit des yeux au derriere
& qu'il s'espargneroit de coups.

28

Did ever noble chatelain
A fairer reputation gain
Defending castles from attack?
And, storming this well-guarded place,
Could the poor boy thrown on his back
Fall rearwards with a better grace?

L'ASSAVT DV CHASTEAV

A ton jamais vû gouverneur
en venir mieux a son honneur
dedans vne ville de guerre ?

G cet autre qu'en cet assaut
ce brave a renversé par terre
pouvoit il faire vn plus beau saut.

29

30 THE VICTIM

I feel quite sorry for this victim,
But though they've rudely cuffed and kicked 'im,
He plans revenge some minutes hence;
If only every hundredth cuff
The boy assigned to his defense
Requites with one, 't will be enough.

This game still survived in the twentieth century at military academies. The winner is the one who can hold on to the cord longest while suffering punishment.

LA POIRE

Ie plains fort ce Soufre-douleur,   Pourveu que des coups qu'il ressent
mais il espere enson malheur   celuy qui veille à sà deffense
tirer raison de cette offense ;   en puisse doner vn pour cent

30

31 BRELAN

While one boy passes with his hoop,
The other children crouch and stoop
And with their cards play games of chance.
The one who thought he'd use the game
His private fortune to enhance
Goes off much lighter than he came.

Brelan was a card game with analogies to poker.

LE BRELAN

Celuy cy roule son Cerceau,
& les autres en vn monceau
des Cartes tentent la fortune ;

Ou tel qui croyoit pour certain
gaigner des autres la pecune,
s'en va leger de plus d'vn grain.

31

All heated by their other games,
They now go off to quench the flames
And in the water have a ball.
Those who don't swim as well as most
Without a dinner drink a toast:
Good health to comrades one and all!

LE BAIN

Tous Eschauffez, des autres Ieux,
Ilz vont, pour esteindre leurs feux,
faire dans l'Eau milles passades;

Ou Souvent, faute de nager,
la plus part boivent, Sans manger,
à la Santé des Camarades.

32

33 SLIDING

Along the ice these children slide;
Their every whim is gratified.
But there's a victim in this farce:
One takes a false step, backward falls;
Another sees him, stops and calls,
"Which one is broken: ice or arse?"

LA GLISSOIRE

Pendant qu'en ce plancher glissant   L'autre, le voyant renversé,
ceux cy se vont divertissant   demande lequel est cassé
l'vn fait vn faux pas en arriere ;   de la Glace, ou de son derriere.

A pastime innocent and tame!
In playing this diverting game
Each couple up and over goes.
But since they squeeze each other tight,
Through malice or through oversight
Ill winds may well assail the nose.

No traditional English name for this game having been located, the descriptive term "Living Wheels" is here used for convenience. In the game of *pet-en-gueule* (or *pète-en-gueule*; "Fart-in-the-face") two boys linked as in the illustration rolled over crouching comrades. A modern form of the game played in school gyms is known in the New York area as "Tanks."

LE IEU DE PET EN GUEULE

Ce plaisir est fort jnnocent,
et dans ce Ieu divertissant
les Enfans se donnent Carriere ;

Mais, côme ils se serrent de pres,
Soit par megarde, ou tout expres,
le nez doit craindre le derriere.

34

35 KNIGHTS

Of these brave jousters in the fray
One pair must lose, one win the day:
You can't avoid this consequence,
Though odds are equal for both sides.
But which one has more common sense,
The horseman or the horse he rides?

In this game of ancient origin one horse and rider team
was out to upset the other.

LA IOVSTE

Que ces Iousteurs ainsy montez,
Seront ou vainqueurs ou domptez,
c'est vne chose jndubitable,

Bienque le party soit egal:
mais quel est le plus raisonable
du Cavalier, ou du cheval. 35

36 STICK TUG

Hunched up and bent, the ground they hug
As on the stick they fiercely tug:
Which one will make the other rise?
But as they squeeze with tight-set mouth,
Beware of thunder from clear skies—
Not from the North but from the South.

Again, we have supplied the English name. The French name means "Short Stick." *Ponant* is actually the West, where the sun *sets*.

LE COVRT BASTON

Ainsy Serrez à croupeton
ils espreuvent au Court Baston
à qui S'enlevera de terre ;

Mais garde que, dans cet effort,
il ne vienne quelque tonerre
plustost du Ponant, que du Nort.

36

37 DICE

This youngster, quite a clever fox,
When suffering from Fortune's knocks
Muddles the dice and plays the thief.
This other boy, who's lost his shirt,
Turns to his bowwow in his grief
To mollify his fiscal hurt.

LES DEZ

Ce Cadet assez raffiné
voyant que la chance à tourné
Broüille les Dez, & les bricolle :

Et cet autre s'en voyant tondu
auec Son Toutou Se console
de tout l'argent qu'il à perdu.

37

38 LEAPFROG

In this spectacular alignment
They leap with luster and refinement,
Some stooping low, some vaulting clear.
And should you be inclined to know
Which one puts on the finest show,
There's no lack of eyeglasses here.

The French name of this variety of leapfrog probably refers to a relay of horses. The "eyeglasses" must surely allude to the numerous paired circular forms in the engraving.

LA POSTE

Ainsy rangez, d'vn air leger
ils S'exercent à voltiger
& vont par voltes & courbettes;

Que si quelqu'vn est curieux
de juger qui Saute le mieux
il n'a pas manque de lunettes. 38

Of cup-and-ball why chatter long?
At best it's just "the same old song."
I much prefer the skill and pleasure
These jumpers are exhibiting
While gaily taking better measure
Than the fair miller with the ring.

La chanson du Ricochet is a traditional French term for a monotonous thing. The "fair miller" with his ring and measure is a folkloristic character.

LE CERCLE ET LE BILBOQVET

A bien parler du Bilboquet   De ces Sauteurs dans le Cerceau;
cest la chanson du Ricochet;   quand ilz preñent mieux leurs mesures
& j'aime bien mieux les postures   que le beau meusnier à l'Aneau.

39

While one contestant cools his heels
The other round the platter wheels,
Buzzing in fly wise as he goes,
And not yet fully satisfied
That the expectant fear of blows
Is not much worse than blows applied.

No English equivalent was located, and no French description that fits this illustration. One version of *mouche* consisted merely of waiting for a fly to settle on one or the other of the two objects at stake.

LA MOVCHE

Pendant qu'il croque le marmot,
l'autre, tournant autour du pot,
Bourdone & contre-fait la mouche ;

N'estant pas encor satisfait,
si la peur qu'on a de la touchè
ne fait plus de mal que l'effet. 40

41 BANDY

Despite the harshness of the weather
These boys come out to play together
And take delight in bandy-ball.
Their ardor does them so much good
And hitting pucks so warms them all,
One stick is worth a stack of wood.

There is a plethora of names for this basic game with a puck and curved sticks, ancestor of hockey, cricket, croquet, lacrosse, golf, shinny, etc.

LA CROSSE

Malgré le temps & la Saison,   & la chacun pour le Degot
ceux cy Sortent de la maison,   S'eschauffe, & dans cet exercice
& s'en vont Crosser par caprice ;   la Crosse leur vaut vn Fagot

41

42 TIPCAT AND PLOWING

Tipcat for some's a timeless joke;
Others, like oxen in a yoke,
Pull a companion through the fields.
But if they had no other bread
Than that their agriculture yields,
They'd surely starve and soon be dead.

LE BATONET ET LA CHARRVE

Le Batonet plaist a ces deux ;
ceux cy couplez comme des Bœufs
traisnent cet autre par les rues :

Mais s'ils n'avoient point d'autre pain
que du labeur de leurs charrues,
ilz pouroient bien mourir de faim. 42

43 SLINGS

Although these scamps on war intent
Employ the very instrument
That loudly through the war has droned,
It surely is a source of joy
That finally this fatal Fronde
Is now a lowly children's toy.

The name *Fronde* (sling) was attached to the sedition
against Mazarin and Anne of Austria, 1648–1652 (thus
ending five years before this collection was published).

LA FRONDE

Bien que ces mauvais garnemens
S'arment des mesmes jnstrumens
qui font tant de Bruit par le mode ;

C'est vn objet divertissant
qu'enfin cette fatalle Fronde
ne soit plus rien qu'vn jeu d'Enfant.

43

44 Darts

Although to see him hold the dart
You'd think him master of his art,
Despite the smirk upon his face
The dart that he is letting fly
Will not land on the wished-for place
So clearly seen with mental eye.

LES DARDS

Bien qu'a luy voir tenir Son Dart   Le trait qu'il Sen va descocher
il paraisse expert en cet Art,   n'ira pas à la mesme place
quelque bonne mine qu'il fasse ;   qu'il Se propose de toucher.

44

45 THE CROSSBOW

Although their shots are sometimes shy
And often merely land nearby,
I'd treat their crossbow with respect,
And know no madman quite so "stark,"
One so devoid of intellect,
Who'd stand and serve them as a mark.

L'ARBALESTE

Quoy qu'ils soient vn peu mal adrets,
qu'ilz donnent souvent par auprés,
j'apprehenderois l'Arbaleste;

& n'en connois point d'assez franc,
ou, si vous voulez, d'assez beste
pour leur aller servir de Blanc 45

46 THE POPINJAY

To emulate the god of love
These tots attack the turtledove,
All in a row and each in turn.
But if they shot such certain darts
As Cupid does to harrow hearts,
With pain her wing would shortly burn.

LE PAPE-GUAY

Ainsy ces enfans tour a tour
vont jmitant le Dieu d'Amour
visant a cette tourterelle ;

Mais s'ilz, Sont aussy bons tireurs,
qu'il S'entend a blesser les cœurs,
elle en aura bientost dans l'aile. 46

47 BALLOON-BALL

This big balloon-ball filled with air
Does often back and forth repair;
A thousand times it whizzes past.
In short, no courier can go
With messages so thick and fast
As this ball travels to and fro.

Note the knobby wooden arm bracers that were often used.

LE BALON

Ce Globe tout enflé de vent
va, court, vient & revient souvent
faisant en l'air mille voyages;

Bref il n'est point de postillon
qui fasse si dru ses messages
qu'ilz en font faire à ce Balon.

47

48 FENCING

Though one is shrewder, in this broil,
In fencing with his little foil,
He can't achieve in any sort
(Since they've no doublets on, you know)
A well-directed tierce or quart
To the ninth button of his foe.

The term *droit dans le bouton* (right on the button) im-
plied a hit executed in perfect form. Presumably the
"ninth button" was the ideal place to hit on the jackets
then in use, but this is uncertain.

L'Escrime

Bien que l'vn semble plus adret
a s'escrimer de son fleuret,
il ne scauroit, quoy qu'il exerce,

N'ayant pourpoint ny hoqueton,
luy dõner de quarte ou de tierce
droit dans le neuviesme bouton.

48

49   Dancing

Whatever pastime you can name,
Could there be found another game
More innocent, more pure and sweet?
And may we not in truth behold
In this array of dancing feet
An image of the age of gold?

LA DANCE

Quelque Ieu qu'on puisse choisir, & ne Semble til pas encor
peut on trouver dans vn plaisir qu'on voit reuiure en cette Dance
plus de douceur & d'innocence ; vne jmage du Siecle d'Or. 49

50 THE BATTLE

This picture shows how party strife
Makes lambkins lead a lion's life,
Destroying all beneath the sun.
And yet the wounded, I suppose,
Left when this hurly-burly's done
Will suffer just a bloody nose.

LA BATAILLE

Voicy comme les Factions
changent les Aigneaux en Lions
G renversent tout Sur la terre.

Mais je croy que po. tous blessez
il restera, de cette guerre,
Seulement quelques nez cassez. 50